READ WOKE BOOKS

LEFT OUT OF HISTORY

THE REAL HISTORY OF JUNETEENTH

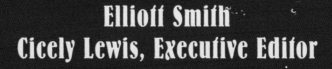

Elliott Smith
Cicely Lewis, Executive Editor

Lerner Publications ◆ Minneapolis

LETTER FROM CICELY LEWIS

CICELY LEWIS

Dear Reader,

It has been said that if we do not learn from our history, we will make the same mistakes. Yet what happens when stories from history are missing, buried, or told from a single viewpoint?

This series sheds light on stories that have been left out of history. As you flip through the pages, you may hear new perspectives you have not heard before. Ask yourself: Who is telling the story? What is their perspective? Why does it matter?

The Read Woke challenge invites readers to question the status quo. I want my students to read books that confront traditional narratives and share stories from underrepresented and oppressed groups. I created Read Woke Books because I want you to be informed and compassionate citizens.

Power to the Reader,

—Cicely Lewis, Executive Editor

TABLE OF CONTENTS

Think critically about the photos and illustrations throughout this book. Who is taking the photos or creating the illustrations? What viewpoint do they represent? How does this affect your viewpoint?

Children celebrate Emancipation Day on August 1, 2011, in Trinidad and Tobago.

FREE AT LAST

Enslavement was a horrible act. Those who enslaved Black people stole labor, knowledge, and life from innocent men, women, and children. Therefore, gaining freedom from enslavement was always a cause for celebration. The festivals across the United States in honor of Juneteenth are examples of this. These celebrations have roots in the past.

In the Caribbean, celebrations began after enslavement ended. Haiti gained its independence from France in 1804. It was the first country to ban slavery.

Emancipation celebrations often include music and dancing, such as this festival in Barbados illustrated circa 1834.

Freedom from British enslavement came for other countries, such as Jamaica and Trinidad and Tobago, in the 1830s. As people gained their freedom, they often used August 1 as the day of celebration. Freed people would take this opportunity to change their names. Surnames had been imposed on them by their enslavers. That is why the last name Freeman became popular during these times.

As more people gained their freedom, other countries also began developing their own celebrations. Many of the traditions started during these festivals are still intact.

FACSIMILE OF THE **Emancipation Proclamation**

Executive Mansion,
Washington, Oct 26. 1863

Ladies having in charge
The North-Western Fair
For the Sanitary Commission
Chicago, Illinois.

According to the request made in your behalf, the original draft of the Emancipation proclamation is herewith enclosed. The formal words at the top, and the conclusion, except the signature, you perceive are not in my hand-writing. They were written at the State Dept. by whom I know not. The printed part was cut from a copy of the preliminary proclamation, and pasted on merely to save writing.

I had some desire to retain the paper; but if it shall contribute to the relief or comfort of the soldiers, that will be better.

Your Obt. Servt.
A. Lincoln

CHAPTER 1
SO WHAT IS JUNETEENTH, ANYWAY?

THE CELEBRATION OF JUNETEENTH IS ROOTED IN SLAVERY. The official end of the enslavement of Black people in the US occurred in 1865 when the Thirteenth Amendment was passed. Two years before that, on January 1, 1863, President Abraham Lincoln signed the Emancipation Proclamation. It declared that most enslaved people within Confederate states were free. The Emancipation Proclamation came two years into the Civil War (1861–1865). The war began as a fight to keep the Northern and Southern states together in spite of disagreements about states' rights and land. White Southerners wanted the right to not only keep slaves but also to bring them into new western territories. However, once Lincoln signed the Emancipation Proclamation, the war turned into a fight for freedom. The Emancipation Proclamation was a historic day for the country. But news did not travel fast in those times.

In Texas, life continued as it was for many people. Enslaved people were still not free. In fact, many enslavers moved to the state to avoid Union troops as the rest of the South

This image shows an artist's view of how the reading of the Emancipation Proclamation may have looked. However, while it was an important step toward freedom from enslavement, the Emancipation Proclamation did not immediately free any slaves.

DiD YOU KNOW?

Enslavement tore apart many families. After freedom, many people attempted to find lost loved ones. They advertised in Black-owned newspapers in search of their relatives. Reunited families celebrated during Juneteenth. These ads still can help people trace their family history.

Lost Friends.

We make no charge for publishing these letters from subscribers. All others will be charged fifty cents. Pastors will please read the requests published below from their pulpits, and report any case where friends are brought together by means of letters in the SOUTHWESTERN.

MR. EDITOR—I wish to inquire for my father; his name is Simon Herd; my name was M. J. Herd; my sister was named Stella Herd. My father belonged to James Johnson, in Jefferson county, Miss., and was sold in time of the war. I was too small to remember who he was sold to. I am married now, and go by the name of M. J. Kennedy. Will the ministers and friends help me to find him? Address me at Pearlington, Miss., care of H. L. Kennedy, pastor In charge of the M. E Church.

M. J. KENNEDY.

Black-owned newspapers ran free ads to help reunite families torn apart by slavery.

Major General Gordon Granger of the Union army

ended slavery. They did this to avoid freeing the people that they enslaved. While some enslavers did not know about the Emancipation Proclamation, others chose not to follow the law. Either way, no one told those enslaved they were free. This went on for more than two years.

Then, on June 19, 1865, federal troops marched into Galveston, Texas. Union general Gordon Granger went around town, reading from General Order No. 3. This order informed those enslaved of the new law. More than 250,000 people were free. But still the law wasn't immediately enforced.

> **"The people of Texas are informed that, in accordance with a proclamation from the Executive of the United States, all slaves are free."**
>
> —GENERAL ORDER NO. 3, 1865

Some enslavers kept the news from the people they enslaved until the work for the season was complete.

For those newly freed, it was a cause for celebration. On the one-year anniversary of their independence, people began hosting Jubilee Day festivities. This marked the beginning of what would become Juneteenth.

REFLECT

More than two years after the Emancipation Proclamation, formerly enslaved people in Texas learned that they were free. What does this say about the power structures? Once Black people learned of their freedom, in what ways were they free? Do you think there were any barriers to their freedom, and if so, what were they?

An Emancipation Day celebration in Richmond, Virginia, 1905

CHAPTER 2
IT STARTED OUT SMALL

FOR MANY YEARS AFTER 1866, JUNETEENTH WAS CELEBRATED PRIMARILY IN TEXAS. Each June 19, people wore their finest clothes and celebrated at a park or other public place. The holiday served as a family reunion. Large groups gathered to recall their family history through enslavement and freedom.

Early Juneteenths featured full readings of the Emancipation Proclamation. Sermons and songs honored the spirituals many enslaved people sang while working. Food was also a major element. Old recipes were preserved, while new food traditions were born at the barbecue pit.

The first celebrations featured an educational component. People learned about their voting rights. And political candidates used the gatherings to gain support.

An Emancipation Day celebration on June 19, 1900, in Austin, Texas

Juneteenth was not without controversy. In the Jim Crow South, many white people fought to end these celebrations. Jim Crow laws prevented Black people from simple freedoms like eating at restaurants or using facilities for white people. One strategy was to ban Black people from gathering in public spaces. But the organizers of Juneteenth celebrations quickly adapted. They began holding festivities near lakes and rivers. Sometimes, people pooled their money and bought the land. Many of these places became known as Emancipation Park.

DiD YOU KNOW?

Foods and drinks at Juneteenth celebrations often have a unique color: red. From red sodas to red velvet cake, the color is a major component of the celebration. Why? Some say red symbolizes the blood of enslaved lives lost. Others say red comes from the African people stolen and forced into slavery. The color was seen as a sign of strength by their ancestors in Africa. While the exact origins of the tradition are unclear, the color red remains present in many Juneteenth celebrations.

This band provided music for the 1900 Juneteenth celebration in Austin, Texas.

Every year, Juneteenth celebrations became more widespread. More cities throughout Texas held gatherings. And as Black people began migrating from the South, they took their traditions with them to their new homes. Slowly, the footprint of Juneteenth spread across the country.

REFLECT

The United States celebrates its independence on July 4. In what ways are the Fourth of July and Juneteenth similar and different? How does your answer depend on your race or ethnicity?

Some Juneteenth celebrations take place in backyards with families, and others bring communities together in public spaces such as this one in Boston.

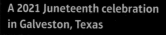
A 2021 Juneteenth celebration in Galveston, Texas

CHAPTER 3
THE FATHER OF JUNETEENTH

OVER ONE HUNDRED YEARS AFTER THE FIRST JUNETEENTH CELEBRATION, BLACK PEOPLE ACROSS TEXAS STILL HONORED TRADITIONS STARTED BY THEIR ANCESTORS. But Texas did not recognize Juneteenth as a holiday. If it fell on a workday or school day, people didn't get the day off.

"This is a holiday not just for Black Texans but for all Texans. This is a day to take pride in our culture and history. Freedom is worth celebrating and I am pleased that we in Texas have been celebrating it for 115 years. I am proud that the celebration is now official and that I had a part in making it so."

—AL EDWARDS,
whose bill made Juneteenth a Texas holiday in 1980

They had to wait until the weekend for the festivities. This did not sit well with Al Edwards, a member of the Texas House of Representatives. Edwards felt that Juneteenth was an important part of state history. He decided to do something about it.

In 1979 Edwards crafted House Bill 1016. The goal of the bill was to make Juneteenth a state holiday. Many of Edwards's fellow legislators argued against the bill. Edwards feared the bill would be defeated. He made several last-minute pleas and deals to get the bill passed.

DiD YOU KNOW?

Black churches played a big role in the development of Juneteenth. These churches formed after slavery ended to offer the newly freed a place to worship. Many early celebrations were held inside Black churches. Soon many churches bought land for celebrating the end of slavery. The churches quickly became a community hub. People learned about current events and politics at church. Decades later, Black churches pushed for expanded Juneteenth celebrations throughout the country.

Throughout history, Black churches have played an important role in Black political action.

On January 1, 1980, House Bill 1016 became law. Texas was the first state to make Juneteenth an officially recognized holiday. Edwards was called the Father of Juneteenth.

A statue in Galveston honors former Texas representative Al Edwards.

Edwards's efforts to honor Juneteenth inspired other advocates. The modern Juneteenth movement began in 1994. Several groups met in New Orleans to organize national Juneteenth celebrations.

Sam Collins stands in front of the Absolute Equality mural in Galveston, Texas. Collins is part of a group working to spread word of the importance of Juneteenth in history.

CHaPTer 4
OPAL LEE PUTS ON HER WALKING SHOES

OPAL LEE WAS BORN IN TEXAS IN 1926. She celebrated Juneteenth with family and friends for many years. After she became a teacher, she helped educate her students about the importance of the day. For years, Lee made it her mission to make Juneteenth a national holiday.

In 2016 Lee took a major step toward her goal. In fact, she took several million steps. Lee decided to walk 1,400 miles (2,253 km) from her home in Texas to Washington, DC, to draw attention to her cause. When Lee started her walk, she was eighty-nine years old! She walked 2.5 miles (4 km) each day to equal the two and a half years it took for those enslaved in Texas to learn of their freedom.

Lee drew excitement everywhere she visited. Along the way, she collected signatures on a petition to make Juneteenth a national holiday. By the time she reached DC in 2017, she had more than one million signatures.

"I decided that surely there was something I could do to bring attention to the fact that we needed Juneteenth as a national holiday. So I decided, if a little old lady in tennis shoes was walking toward Washington, DC, somebody would take notice."

—OPAL LEE, ON HER WALK

Opal Lee worked for many years to make Juneteenth a national holiday.

As the US struggled with social justice issues in 2020, more non-Black people realized how important Juneteenth was in the Black community. Some companies began giving employees the day off. And momentum for Lee's dream continued to grow.

In June 2021, Lee witnessed history. President Joe Biden signed a law making Juneteenth a national holiday. Biden honored Lee during the ceremony. Juneteenth is the first new federal holiday since Martin Luther King Jr. Day was created

Five years after Opal Lee's historic walk, community members celebrate the first official US Juneteenth holiday by marching through Fort Worth.

in 1983. Thanks to the efforts of people like Lee, what was once a small, regional celebration has become a chance for everyone to learn an important history lesson.

President Joe Biden signed the Juneteenth National Independence Day Act into law in 2021 as Vice President Kamala Harris (*front row, third from left*) and Opal Lee (*front row, second from left*) look on.

REFLECT

When Juneteenth became a national holiday, every state except South Dakota recognized it as a holiday. Provide an argument for or against making Juneteenth a holiday.

WAYS TO CELEBRATE JUNETEENTH

GATHER — Join or host a Juneteenth cookout or parade.

EDUCATE — Teach someone who doesn't know about the history of Juneteenth.

SERVE — Volunteer in the Black community.

LISTEN — Speak to or interview a Black elder about their history with Juneteenth.

CONNECT AND REFLECT

Consider the way this book tells the story of Juneteenth. Think about an important event in your life. How would you tell a friend about it? How might that story be different if another person told it? Why is it important who tells a story?

GLOSSARY

ADVOCATE: a person who speaks in support of something

ELDER: a person who is older

EMANCIPATION: to set free from slavery

LEGISLATOR: a lawmaker

MIGRATING: moving from one region to another

PETITION: a formal, written request by many people

PLEA: a request for help

PROCLAMATION: to announce in public

SERMON: a speech intended to teach

SURNAME: the family or last name

SOURCE NOTES

10   Teresa Palomo Acosta, "Juneteenth," Texas State Historical Association, June 30, 2021, https://www.tshaonline.org/handbook /entries/juneteenth.

17   Al Edwards, "Al Edwards Juneteenth Statement," June 1, 1980, available online at Oak Park (IL) Public Library, https://www.oppl .org/wp-content/uploads/2020/06/Al-Edwards-Juneteenth -Statement.pdf.

22   Manseen Logan, "92-Year-Old Ms. Opal Lee Walks It Like She Talks It to Make Juneteenth a National Holiday," Blavity, June 13, 2019, https://blavity.com/blavity-original/92-year-old-ms-opal-lee -walks-it-like-she-talks-it-to-make-juneteenth-a-national-holiday ?category1=culture.

READ WOKE READING LIST

Celebrating Juneteenth: *National Geographic Kids*
https://kids.nationalgeographic.com/history/article
/celebrating-juneteenth

Dolbear, Emily. *Juneteenth*. Mankato, MN: Child's World, 2021.

Duncan, Alice Faye. *Opal Lee and What It Means to Be Free: The True Story of the Grandmother of Juneteenth*. Nashville: Tommy Nelson, 2022.

Green, Amanda Jackson. *Hidden Black History: From Juneteenth to Redlining*. Minneapolis: Lerner Publications, 2021.

Jewel, Kirsti. *What Is Juneteenth?* New York: Penguin Workshop, 2022.

Juneteenth: Britannica
https://kids.britannica.com/students/article/Juneteenth/632534

Juneteenth (Children's Edition)
https://www.blackpast.org/childrens-page/juneteenth/

A Juneteenth Celebration: *Time for Kids*
https://www.timeforkids.com/g56/a-juneteenth-celebration/

INDEX

PHOTO ACKNOWLEDGMENTS

Image credits: Salim October/Shutterstock, p. 4; The Print Collector/Heritage Images/Getty Images, p. 5; Science History Images/Alamy Stock Photo, p. 6; Library of Congress, pp. 7, 11; The Historic New Orleans Collection, p. 8; Hi-Story/Alamy Stock Photo, p. 9; The Portal to Texas History Austin History Center, Austin Public Library, p. 12; The Portal to Texas History, University of North Texas Libraries, p. 14; Boston Globe/Getty Images, pp. 15, 19; Go Nakamura/Stringer/Getty Images, p. 16; Schomburg Center for Research in Black Culture, Photographs and Prints Division, The New York Public Library, p. 18; Francois Picard/Getty Images, p. 20; Bastiaan Slabbers/Getty Images, p. 21; AP Photo/Amanda McCoy, pp. 23, 24; Carlos Fyfe/The White House, p. 25; AlliesTroop/Shutterstock, p. 26; Probal Rashid/LightRocket/Getty Images, p. 27. Design elements: Ursa Major/Shutterstock; Mint Images/Getty Images; Jose A. Bernat Bacete/Moment/Getty Images.

Cover: Library of Congress; The Portal to Texas History, University of North Texas Libraries.

Content consultant: Cleopatra Warren, PhD, Secondary Social Studies Instructor, Atlanta Public Schools

Lerner Publications Company
An imprint of Lerner Publishing Group, Inc.
241 First Avenue North
Minneapolis, MN 55401 USA

For reading levels and more information, look up this title at www.lernerbooks.com.

Main body text set in Aptifer Sans LT Pro.
Typeface provided by Linotype AG.

Editor: Amber Ross **Designer:** Viet Chu **Photo Editor:** Annie Zheng
Lerner team: Martha Kranes

Library of Congress Cataloging-in-Publication Data

Names: Smith, Elliott, 1976– author.
Title: The real history of Juneteenth / Elliott Smith.
Description: Minneapolis : Lerner Publications, [2023] | Series: Left out of history (read woke books) | Includes bibliographical references and index. | Audience: Ages 9–11 | Audience: Grades 4–6 | Summary: "Juneteenth is the celebration of the day enslaved people in Texas were told they were freed. This book explores Juneteenth's little-told history, from the first Jubilee to the making of a national holiday"— Provided by publisher.
Identifiers: LCCN 2022008730 (print) | LCCN 2022008731 (ebook) | ISBN 9781728475837 (lib. bdg.) | ISBN 9781728479095 (pbk.) | ISBN 9781728482903 (eb pdf)
Subjects: LCSH: Juneteenth—Juvenile literature. | African Americans—Texas—History—Juvenile literature. | Slaves—Emancipation—United States—Juvenile literature. | African Americans—Anniversaries, etc.—Juvenile literature.
Classification: LCC E185.93.T4 S54 2023 (print) | LCC E185.93.T4 (ebook) | DDC 394.263—dc23/eng/20220222

LC record available at https://lccn.loc.gov/2022008730
LC ebook record available at https://lccn.loc.gov/2022008731

Manufactured in the United States of America
1-52150-50613-6/22/2022